EGG PAINTING
AND DECORATING

EGG PAINTING
AND DECORATING

20 enchanting ideas for creating beautiful displays

Deborah Schneebeli-Morrell

Photographs by Heini Schneebeli

southwater

DEDICATION
TO THE MEMORY OF CHRISTINE WALKER, A
WONDERFUL FRIEND AND TEACHER.

This edition is published by Southwater

Southwater is an imprint of Anness Publishing Ltd,
Hermes House, 88–89 Blackfriars Road, London
SE1 8HA; tel. 020 7401 2077; fax 020 7633 9499
www.southwaterbooks.com;
www.annesspublishing.com

If you like the images in this book and would
like to investigate using them for publishing,
promotions or advertising, please visit our website
www.practicalpictures.com for more information.

© Anness Publishing Ltd 1997, 2007

UK agent: The Manning Partnership Ltd;
tel. 01225 478444; fax 01225 478440;
sales@manning-partnership.co.uk

UK distributor: Grantham Book Services Ltd;
tel. 01476 541080; fax 01476 541061;
orders@gbs.tbs-ltd.co.uk

North American agent/distributor: National Book
Network; tel. 301 459 3366; fax 301 429 5746;
www.nbnbooks.com

Australian agent/distributor: Pan Macmillan
Australia; tel. 1300 135 113; fax 1300 135 103;
customer.service@macmillan.com.au

New Zealand agent/distributor: David Bateman Ltd;
tel. (09) 415 7664; fax (09) 415 8892

Publisher: Joanna Lorenz
Project Editor: Joanna Bentley
Photographer: Heini Schneebeli
Stylist: Deborah Schneebeli-Morrell
Designer: Peter Butler

ETHICAL TRADING POLICY
Because of our ongoing ecological investment
programme, you, as our customer, can have the
pleasure and reassurance of knowing that a tree is
being cultivated on your behalf to naturally replace
the materials used to make the book you are holding.
For further information about this scheme, go to
www.annesspublishing.com/trees

Previously published as *The Decorative Egg Book*

Main front cover image shows Primary Dipped Eggs
– for project, see page 18

CONTENTS

INTRODUCTION

The form of the egg, an elongated sphere, is one of the most beautiful shapes that occurs in nature. The symmetrical form lends itself to decoration, giving rise to the great variety of decorative patterns and techniques used on eggs, found most prominently in folk cultures around the world.

As one of the most ancient universal symbols, the egg appears throughout history and in the disparate and varied cultures of peoples from every continent. As a readily understandable symbol for life, it features prominently in creation myths where it symbolizes the very beginnings of time as if it were the world itself, enclosing the mystery of life within.

The egg commonly appears in religious rituals and customs throughout the world: a roasted egg is prepared for the Jewish festival of Passover to represent a burnt offering and as a symbol of hope in the midst of the persecution of the Jews in ancient Egypt. The Maoris in New Zealand placed an egg in the hand of a dead person before burial, perhaps in the expectation of a swift voyage to a new episode in life's journey. In China, eggs have traditionally been used in temple offerings.

The strength of an egg as a power for good means that it has been used in many cultures as a protection against the evil eye, to ward off lightning and to cure illness. It was said that if a woman found a double yolk on breaking an egg, good luck and fertility would follow. In England, it was a custom to keep the last egg from an old hen as a talisman, and in Germany it was common to swear an oath on an egg.

Ostrich eggs are frequently found hanging in churches, monasteries and mosques all over the Middle

The techniques and colours of traditional folk art work particularly well on the smooth symmetry of the egg.

East and North Africa. They are thought to be symbols of God's watchful care. Ostriches are forgetful birds and legend has it that they hatch their eggs by watching them, and if they turn away the eggs addle. They are therefore used to remind worshippers how easy it is to forget God.

Eggs often appear in fairy stories, the most famous being *The Goose that Laid the Golden Egg* from Grimm's Fairy Tales.

In the West, egg customs and the giving of eggs are now most widely associated with Easter. The name Easter derives from the Anglo-Saxon name *Eastre*, the pagan goddess of spring and fertility. Spring, when Easter falls, was a most important time in the pagan calendar and, as so often happens, a Christian festival is coincidentally celebrated at the same time as an earlier pagan one. This pagan festival celebrates the death of winter, the relinquishing of a barren season, and the egg is a potent symbol to signify the rebirth of nature at springtime.

The practice of giving chocolate eggs at Easter is a relatively recent one, and exquisite examples are created by imaginative confectioners, particularly in central Europe. There are also many traditions of decorating and giving real eggs at this time, and decorating eggs has become a wonderful vehicle for exhibiting artistic skills to family and friends.

The Ukranian and Czechoslovakian batik eggs are beautifully patterned and coloured, while the freehand sgraffito eggs from Bavaria and Switzerland often have outstandingly intricate designs. The Polish technique of using cut and coloured paper to decorate an egg is beautifully effective and surprisingly easy to do. Simple folk painting and decorative techniques were often borrowed from other applications and applied to the surface of an egg to create unusual and stunning results.

Although some techniques are more intricate and specialised, requiring some degree of skill to execute, others are simpler both in the use of technique and materials. For example, boiling an egg in a dye bath of onion skins can produce lovely rich oranges and browns. Similarly, simple stencils can be used to mask an area of the eggshell which is then dyed and the stencil removed to leave an effective negative design. One of the most common examples of this method is using real leaves as the stencil – a magical process simple enough for a child to do.

Many of the projects in this book use traditional and well-tried methods of decoration such as the sgraffito designs on dyed eggs using images from folk art, real leaf stencilling using natural dyes or decorating the shell of the egg with leaves and flowers cut from coloured paper.

Most of the projects use natural eggs: hen, bantam, pullet, duck, quail and even an ostrich egg. Most eggs are relatively easy to find although you may have to search a little harder for an ostrich egg.

Almost all the projects in this book may be carried out on either blown or hard-boiled eggs. Decorating a hard-boiled egg makes it a delight to serve at table, but if you can't bear to see your creation destroyed when eaten and you want to keep your eggs indefinitely, then it is best to blow them first.

Above: *Gilt creams produce stunning results on hens' eggs.*

Right: *In their natural form, freshly gathered eggs are a delight to look at.*

EGG GUIDE

The egg is a beautiful shape and as such is a natural object for decoration. The range of colours, sizes and patterning in the infinite variety of eggs is unique and so only a number of the most suitable have been chosen for the projects in this book. Eggs are a delight to look at, hold and feel even before they are transformed by decoration. We seem to get a kind of ancient satisfaction from viewing a nest of eggs or collecting a basket of freshly laid hens' eggs, as if harking back to a time when all our food came from the natural world.

All the eggs in this book are easy to find, but you will probably only find brown hens' eggs and possibly quails' eggs in a supermarket. Pullet, bantam and white hens' eggs are more likely to be found in a farmshop along with duck or goose eggs. Some traditional butchers stock these last two varieties. An ostrich egg is more diffi-cult to find, but junk shops and antique markets are a good source, along with some decorative house-style shops.

Duck eggs: Beautiful eggs in either white or pale blue. The shell is particularly smooth and takes dye and paint well. They are much larger than hens' eggs and the shell is very strong so they are suitable for blowing. They are the eggs most often used in this book. They are often dirty so need to be washed well – ducks tend to paddle around in mud a lot!

Goose eggs: Elongated and very white. As they are so much larger than other eggs, they are naturally stronger.

Hens' eggs: Either brown or white. Brown eggs are the most popular, in the mistaken view that they are healthier and better to eat. The truth is that there is no difference at all in the nutritional quality between brown and white eggs. As a general rule, white hens lay white eggs and brown hens lay brown eggs. The real difference is between factory-farmed eggs and free-range organic eggs, the latter being infinitely tastier and also having stronger shells – ideal for decorating. Small breeds of hen, such as bantams, produce little eggs in varying colours. Pullets are young hens and therefore produce small eggs.

White duck eggs (in blue egg rack), blue duck eggs (in mortar), ostrich egg (on paper) and goose eggs (in blue-rimmed basket).

used in this book. The shells are very thin and fragile, so care must be taken when blowing them; don't use an egg pump for these.

Wooden eggs: Available in different sizes, either from mail order craft catalogues or from gift shops. They are sometimes painted but this doesn't matter for the decoupage project, as the decoration you apply will cover them completely.

Left: *Polystyrene eggs and wooden eggs are available in many different sizes, making it easy to find the right one for any project.*

Below: *Bantam eggs (back row left), brown hens' eggs (in large centre basket), pullets' eggs (in basket with birch bark handle), white hens' eggs (front row, basket with ivy leaf), quails' eggs (spilling out on to moss).*

Ostrich eggs: Immensely strong and completely different in quality and character from all the other eggs. The ostrich is an enormous, flightless bird which roams the plains of Africa and lays the largest egg that appears in nature. The eggs have a strange and exotic feel with a finely pitted and subtly polished ivory-coloured shell. Suitable for single displays.

Polystyrene (Styrofoam) eggs: Useful for beading projects when pins with beads on can be pushed into the egg shape. They can be bought in several sizes.

Quails' eggs: These speckly eggs are the most wild looking of the egg types

EQUIPMENT AND MATERIALS

You really don't need much in the way of specialist tools or equipment to prepare eggs for decoration. In fact, you will probably have most things in your home already.

EQUIPMENT

Cloths: Odd bits of soft clean cloth are useful for giving eggs a good polish after decoration.

Craft knife: Use one with a retractable blade for the sgraffito projects. It is very safe to use and enables you to work much more easily with a small part of the blade extended.

Drawing tools: Fine felt-tip pens, a white pencil and a soft graphite pencil are needed to draw around templates and to mark designs on to the egg before decoration.

Dressmaker's tracing wheel: A useful tool that produces a pretty raised pattern on copper foil.

Egg blowing kit: Comprises a small plastic pump and a tiny drill. It's not essential, but it does make blowing eggs a lot easier and is available from a mail order craft supplier.

Egg carton: Handy for resting eggs on when they have been taken out of the dye and need to dry.

Jars and bowls: A good assortment of these is needed for mixing synthetic dyes along with some plastic food tubs with lids.

Paintbrushes: These are required for paint, glue, gold size and gilt cream as well as varnish.

Pair of tights: Cut up an old pair of tights to use in stencilling projects.

Pinking shears: Useful for cutting zig-zagged edges on coloured paper or copper foil.

Plastic syringe: Useful to push soapy water into the egg to clean the inside and for filling the egg with water to help it submerge in the dye. They are easy to find at a chemist's.

Scissors: A large pair for general cutting and a small, pointed pair for more intricate cutting are required.

Slotted spoon: Useful for putting the eggs into a saucepan of dye and for lifting them out again.

Stainless steel saucepan: Ideal for mixing and heating natural dyes.

Steel wool: Use fine gauge steel wool to create a distressed effect on gold leaf projects.

Wire egg rack: Made by threading firm wire through previously drilled holes in a thin piece of wood and used for holding blown eggs.

MATERIALS

The large variety of decorative techniques used in this book means that you need quite a large selection of materials. All the projects are inexpensive to make despite the fact that some end up looking very precious indeed.

You will probably find you already have the basic equipment for egg decorating.

Acrylic paints: A selection of a small amount of good quality paints is needed for the painting projects.

Beads: A varied selection of small iridescent glass beads is required.

Bleach: Used to remove dye, this is readily available, but must only be used in small quantities and with care.

Copper wire: Used to attach eggs to each other.

Dressmaker's pins: Necessary for sticking beads into polystyrene eggs.

Embroidery threads: A selection of cotton embroidery threads can be used to decorate eggs in stripes and spirals.

Gilt cream: From specialist art shops.

Glue: The projects use PVA (white) glue, which is very adaptable; fungicide-free wallpaper paste, which is excellent for paper projects; and paper glue.

Gold leaf: Available at specialist art shops.

Japan gold size: Varnish to which gold leaf is stuck. Available at specialist art shops.

Natural dyes: Can be ordered from a mail order craft catalogue (except for onion skins which are easy to collect). The natural wood dyes come in the form of fine wood chippings and are the same dyes that are used in wool and yarn dyeing, so they may be available from a specialist shop.

Paper: Origami paper is ideal for paper-cutting projects, or you can use poster paper.

Red bole: Traditional undercoat for gold leaf. From specialist art shops.

Synthetic Easter egg dyes: Available from a good craft shop or a mail order craft catalogue.

With a good supply of beautifully coloured papers, paints and dyes, you're ready to start transforming your eggs.

BASIC TECHNIQUES

The projects in this book are very accessible – all you need is enthusiasm, deft fingers and occasional patience.

A variety of techniques and approaches to decoration are involved; some are traditional methods, long used in the art of egg decoration, and others are well-known decorative finishes cleverly applied to the enticing surface of an egg.

As you develop confidence and enthusiasm, you will no doubt extend and adapt the projects to suit your own style or even perhaps combine one or two techniques to produce a new idea. This, after all, is the nature of the creative process.

The basic techniques, particularly in the preparation of eggs prior to decoration, are outlined below.

Boiling eggs: To ensure that the eggs don't crack while boiling, it is best to pierce the air sack at the larger end of the egg with a fine needle. Don't put the eggs directly into boiling water and never boil them rapidly. You can simply preserve such eggs by applying two coats of varnish to seal them.

Blowing eggs traditionally: Pierce either end of the egg with a sharp needle; the end with the air sack should be pierced with a larger hole. Put the egg to your lips and blow firmly through the top hole so that the contents flow out of the larger hole at the base. Catch the contents in a bowl and if the eggs are fresh, use them in the kitchen.

Blowing eggs with a kit: If you want to blow larger quantities of eggs, it is best to invest in an egg blowing kit consisting of a drill and a small pump. The advantage of this kit, apart from you not feeling dizzy, is that you just make one hole in the egg with the drill, insert the pump and pump in the air via a fine tube.

1 *Push the drill into the base of the egg and twist it around to make a neat hole, big enough for the pump.*

2 *Push the pump into the hole and pump air into the egg gently. The contents will flow out of the hole steadily until the egg is empty.*

Threading eggs on to ribbon:

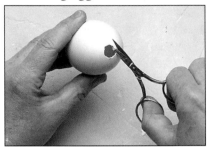

Enlarging the blowhole at either end of the egg with small pointed scissors makes it possible to thread the egg on to a wide ribbon.

Cleaning the inside of an egg: The inside of the egg can be cleaned by injecting soapy water into the hole with a plastic syringe; this can then be pumped out.

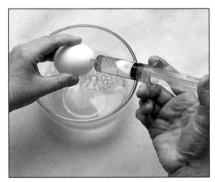

Fill the syringe with warm soapy water and pump it into the hole in the egg. Shake the egg gently to clean the inside and flush the water out with an egg pump.

Filling blown eggs with water: To make blown eggs submerge in a dye bath, you need to fill them with liquid. Either hold them under the dye until all the air is released or, for a quicker method, fill the egg with water first using a small syringe.

Washing eggs: It is always best to wash eggs before decorating, especially if they are going to be dyed or painted, and ducks' eggs, for instance, can be really dirty.

Wash eggs in warm soapy water and gently clean off all grease and dirt with a soft scouring pad.

Using natural dyes: These dyes are easy to use. Wear rubber gloves if you worry about getting coloured hands. Natural dyes are unpredictable and can vary a lot in tone, so experiment to obtain the strength of colour you require. Onion skins are used in one of the projects and other foods such as spinach, beetroot and tea can also be very effective – experimentation is the name of the game.

Spoon the natural dyes into a stainless steel saucepan, cover with water and bring to the boil; the longer it boils before the eggs are put in, the stronger the colour will be.

Using synthetic dyes: Synthetic dyes should be used according to the manufacturer's instructions. They are generally mixed in glass jars and the eggs are lowered into the dye with a spoon.

1 *Mix the required amount of dye in a glass jar and dye the eggs one at a time. Put them in and take them out with a metal spoon.*

2 *After the required strength of colour has been reached, remove the egg from the jar and dry it in an egg box.*

Drying eggs: When you need to dry the egg after painting, dyeing or decorating, use either an old egg box, some folded kitchen paper or, for blown eggs, put them on to an egg rack.

Remove the blown eggs from the dye, drain and dry them upside down on an egg rack.

15

ONION SKIN EGGS

This is one of the simplest techniques in the book – brown hens' eggs are boiled in a saucepan of dye made from onion skins to produce a rich orange-brown colour. The onion skins need to be boiled previously in a saucepan of water to release their colour; the colour can be deepened by adding red onion skins to the water. Freshly boiled eggs can be served for breakfast using this method, although to obtain a deeper colour it would be best to hard-boil the eggs.

EQUIPMENT AND MATERIALS
- LARGE HANDFUL OF ONION SKINS
- STAINLESS STEEL SAUCEPAN
- BROWN HENS' EGGS
- SLOTTED SPOON
- METAL SCOURING PAD

1 Put the onion skins in a pan three-quarters full of water. Bring to the boil and simmer for five to ten minutes to release the colour. Place the eggs in the pan, topping up the water level to cover them, and boil gently; four minutes for soft-boiled eggs with a light colour or ten minutes for hard-boiled eggs with a deeper colour.

2 Remove the eggs from the pan with a slotted spoon, cool under cold running water and, while they are still wet, scratch them firmly all over with a scouring pad.

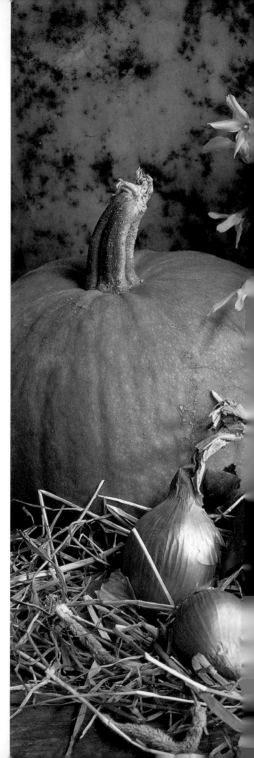

PRIMARY DIPPED EGGS

These brightly coloured, hard-boiled hens' eggs are simple enough for a child to make. The warm boiled egg is simply submerged in the synthetic dye for about ten minutes. Arrange the finished eggs on a table in a cheerful nest strewn with mouthwatering chocolate praline eggs, or wrap them in shimmering coloured net tied with a matching satin ribbon.

EQUIPMENT AND MATERIALS
- EASTER EGG DYE: RED, YELLOW AND BLUE
- 3 GLASS JARS
- WHITE HENS' EGGS, HARD-BOILED AND STILL WARM
- TEASPOON
- KITCHEN PAPER OR EGG CARTON

1 Mix the three dyes in the jars according to the manufacturer's instructions.

2 Place a warm egg into each jar and leave for about ten minutes, or until the shell has taken on the required colour. Remove the egg and leave it to dry on kitchen paper or in an egg carton.

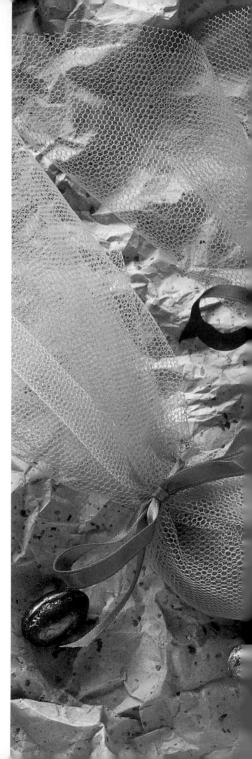

LEAF STENCILS

*T*his simple project produces *magical results using perfect little newly emerged spring leaves. Small flowers are ideal as well. The trick is to lay the leaf really flat against the surface of the egg and then tie the band of tights very firmly to secure the leaf. Blown white duck eggs are used here, and the hole at either end of the egg is enlarged with small pointed scissors to enable the finished eggs to be threaded prettily on to a sumptuous wide ribbon.*

EQUIPMENT AND MATERIALS
- LARGE WHITE DUCK EGGS, BLOWN
- SELECTION OF FRESHLY PICKED LEAVES
- SCISSORS
- OLD TIGHTS, CUT INTO 20 CM (8 IN) BANDS
- RUBBER BANDS
- NATURAL DYES: LOGWOOD AND YELLOW WOOD MIXED WITH MATE TEA
- STAINLESS STEEL SAUCEPAN ,
- SLOTTED SPOON
- KITCHEN PAPER

1 Wet the surface of the egg and carefully position an opened-out leaf on to the side.

2 Carefully wrap a band made from old tights around the egg, pull tightly and secure with a rubber band.

3 Mix the dye in a pan (two spoons of dye to a pan of water), boil for ten minutes and then add the eggs. Fill the eggs with water so they submerge. Boil for about 30 minutes, or until the shell has taken on the required colour.

4 Remove the eggs from the pan when they are the colour you want, and cool under cold running water. Cut open the tights at the back of the egg and remove. Peel off the leaf to reveal the undyed shell beneath.

DIP-DYED TARTAN

This method produces a really beautiful design and although these eggs take a little while to make, they are not difficult. The technique of over-dipping the colours means many more shades are created than dyes used. It is best to use white hen or duck eggs. For this project they have been hard-boiled, but if you want to keep the eggs for longer, you can use blown eggs.

EQUIPMENT AND MATERIALS
- 3 PLASTIC FOOD TUBS
- MARKER PEN
- SCISSORS
- EASTER EGG DYE: BLUE, RED AND YELLOW
- LARGE WHITE HEN OR DUCK EGGS, HARD-BOILED AND STILL WARM
- KITCHEN PAPER

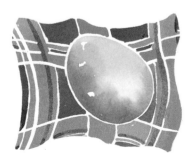

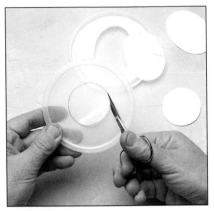

1 Trace the templates from the back of the book and trace them on to the tub lids. Cut around them.

2 Mix the three dyes in the three tubs according to the manufacturer's instructions. Place the lids on top with the circular shape on the blue dye.

3 Place a warm egg upright into the circular hole of the blue dye. Leave for about ten minutes, or until the shell has taken on the required colour. Remove the egg and wipe off any drips of dye. Turn the egg upside down and repeat the process. Leave to dry.

4 Place the egg sideways into the oval hole of the red dye. Repeat with the other side. Finally dip the remaining long sides of the egg into the yellow dye.

DUCKS' CROWNS

S tart the day with these regal pale blue duck eggs. The lustrous girdles and the little copper crowns can be used time and time again. Copper is a particularly rewarding metal to work with – it is soft and easy to cut and calls for no special skills. Children love to have a go with this material.

EQUIPMENT AND MATERIALS
- PINKING SHEARS
- .003 GAUGE COPPER FOIL, 25 CM X 25 CM (10 IN X 10 IN)
- DRESSMAKER'S TRACING WHEEL
- DOUBLE-SIDED TAPE
- SMALL, SHARP SCISSORS
- CARD (STOCK)
- BLUE DUCK EGGS, LIGHTLY BOILED

1 With pinking shears, cut two lengths of copper foil about 1 cm (½ in) wide; one to fit around the egg lengthways and the other widthways. Make two parallel lines down the centre of each copper strip by rolling the tracing wheel along each edge.

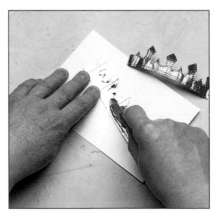

3 Place the copper crown on a piece of card and decorate it with the tracing wheel.

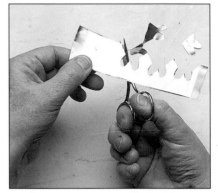

2 Trace the crown template from the back of the book and tape it to a piece of copper foil. Cut around the template and remove it.

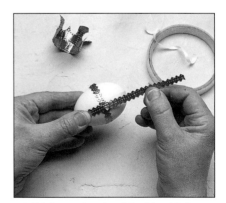

4 Stick two bands of double-sided tape around the egg width and length. Place the copper bands on top, press down and trim off any excess length. Bend the crown around on itself, overlap one end and secure with tape. Place the crown on top of the egg.

SPOTTY EASTER WANDS

Blown bantam and pullet eggs are decorated with brightly coloured polka dots using a selection of good felt-tip pens. The ones used here are spirit-based, waterproof and of course easy to use as they dry immediately. The vibrant colours of the eggs, complemented by the brilliant tones of the dyed feathers when threaded together on copper wire, make these wands witty and entertaining Easter decorations.

EQUIPMENT AND MATERIALS
- 3 BANTAM OR PULLET EGGS, BLOWN
- NEEDLE
- SPIRIT-BASED FELT-TIP PENS: ORANGE, BRIGHT PINK, YELLOW AND PURPLE
- PLIERS
- TWO LENGTHS COPPER WIRE, EACH 40 CM (16 IN)
- 3 EACH OF GREEN, BLUE AND PINK FEATHERS
- PVA (WHITE) GLUE

1 Make a hole in each end of the eggs with a needle. Draw large orange dots over one egg, then colour the surrounding area in bright pink. Colour another egg yellow with pink dots and the third one purple with yellow dots.

2 Using the pliers, bend one end of a piece of wire into a spiral and thread the eggs on to it.

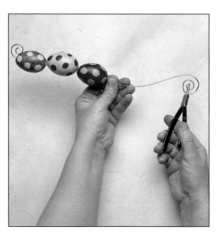

3 Turn the other end of the wire into a slightly larger spiral.

4 Dip the ends of the green feathers into PVA glue and push them into the hole at the top of the first egg. Secure the egg and the feathers to the wire with the glue. Repeat this process with the blue and pink feathers.

STRIPY EGGS

These striking hard-boiled duck eggs would make an entertaining addition to an Easter picnic. Imagine the surprise of the picnickers when you open a plain egg box and reveal such delights. The technique is similar to the traditional batik method – part of the shell is masked off with masking fluid and the egg is dyed in a pan of natural dye. The masking fluid is then removed to reveal the shining white shell underneath that contrasts so beautifully with the coloured stripes.

EQUIPMENT AND MATERIALS
- WHITE DUCK EGGS
- MASKING FLUID
- FINE PAINTBRUSH
- NATURAL DYES: LOGWOOD, REDWOOD AND YELLOW WOOD
- STAINLESS STEEL SAUCEPAN
- SLOTTED SPOON

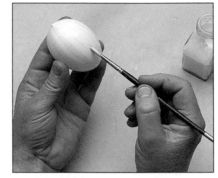

1 Paint bold stripes on to the eggs with the masking fluid. The stripes should be wider in the middle and taper off at each end. Leave to dry thoroughly.

2 Meanwhile mix the dye in a pan (two spoons to a pan of water), boil for ten minutes and then place the eggs in, ensuring they are fully covered. Boil for about ten minutes, or until the shells have taken on the required colour. Remove the eggs from the pan, rinse off the bits of dye under cold running water and remove the masking fluid.

AFRICAN RESIST

The technique and design of these beautiful indigo-dyed duck eggs have been inspired by African textiles with their bold pattern and restrained colour. The method is the same as the Stripy Eggs project but the final effect is entirely different. Large white and pale blue duck eggs are used. They have been hard-boiled, but if you want to keep them longer, then use blown eggs.

EQUIPMENT AND MATERIALS
- WHITE AND BLUE DUCK EGGS, HARD-BOILED OR BLOWN
- MASKING FLUID
- FINE PAINTBRUSH
- BLUE EASTER EGG DYE
- BOWL
- SLOTTED SPOON
- EGG CARTON

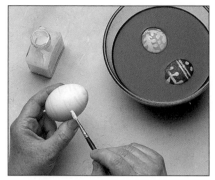

1 Paint two concentric bands around each end of the eggs with the masking fluid. Leave to dry thoroughly before painting on the "leaves" in the centre and the dots at either end. Leave to dry. Meanwhile mix the dye in a bowl according to the manufacturer's instructions and add the eggs.

2 Leave the eggs in the dye until the shells have taken on the required colour, then transfer to an egg carton. Remove the masking fluid from each egg to reveal the contrasting pattern.

GOLDEN EGGS

*T*hese fairy-tale eggs with their gently glimmering finish make precious gifts that can be kept for ever. Gilding with gold or precious metal leaf is not as difficult as it looks, nor is it as expensive as it might seem. The eggs with the more textured finish are gilded with patinated copper leaf which is usually available from specialist art shops along with the more common gold and silver leaf. Artificial gold leaf is a less expensive alternative.

EQUIPMENT AND MATERIALS
- RED BOLE OR RED-OXIDE GESSO
- PAINTBRUSH
- HENS' EGGS, BLOWN
- SCISSORS
- JAPAN GOLD SIZE
- GOLD LEAF, CUT IN SMALL SQUARES
- SOFT PAINTBRUSH
- FINE STEEL WOOL
- SOFT CLOTH (OPTIONAL)

1 Paint the red bole on to the egg. You will have to do this in two halves so that you can hold the egg, allowing the bole to dry between each.

2 Paint half of the egg with gold size. When it is almost dry, but still tacky, stick the small squares of gold leaf all around the egg, metal-side down. Leave to dry and repeat on the other side. Leave to dry overnight.

3 Clean off the overlapping bits of gold by brushing them off with a soft paintbrush. The egg should be evenly covered.

4 Rub the egg very gently with fine steel wool to create a distressed effect. Alternatively, rub with a soft cloth for a shiny finish.

BLEACHED SPIRALS

This simple project uses a well-known traditional technique. Very intricate designs can be created using both brushes and dip pens. The simple and popular spiral motif is an ideal starting point and it is an easy way of making an all-over pattern. Only use the tiniest amount of bleach, don't let it touch your skin, and work in a well-ventilated space. White hens' eggs are used here but duck eggs would be equally suitable.

EQUIPMENT AND MATERIALS
- EGG DRILL
- WHITE HENS' EGGS
- BOWL
- NATURAL DYES: LOGWOOD AND WALNUT SHELL
- STAINLESS STEEL SAUCEPAN
- SLOTTED SPOON
- BLEACH
- EGG CUP
- FINE PAINTBRUSH
- KITCHEN PAPER

1 Using the egg drill, make a hole in the larger end of the egg, insert the pump and gently pump out the contents into a bowl. Wash out the egg.

2 Put 2 tablespoons of each dye in a pan three-quarters full of water, boil, then add the egg. Ensure that the egg is fully covered and leave it in the dye until the shell becomes very dark.

3 Pour some bleach into an egg cup and paint the spirals on to the egg. Paint a dot between each spiral. Leave for about 30 seconds to allow the bleach to eat away at the dyed surface.

4 Wipe away the bleach with kitchen paper to reveal the white surface below the dye.

SGRAFFITO

*S*graffito is the term used to
describe scratching through one
colour to reveal the colour beneath, in
this case the white eggshell. This style
of egg is very popular in Switzerland
and southern Germany. A little care
and patience is needed to work this
technique but the method is really
quite simple. Natural dyes are used
to complement the folk art imagery,
but an altogether different effect could
be achieved by scratching the design
over brighter synthetic colours. Duck
eggs must be used as their shells are
much stronger.

EQUIPMENT AND MATERIALS
- EGG DRILL
- WHITE DUCK EGGS
- BOWL
- LOGWOOD DYE
- STAINLESS STEEL SAUCEPAN
- SLOTTED SPOON
- WHITE PENCIL
- CRAFT KNIFE

▶

1 Using the egg drill, make a hole in the larger end of the egg, insert the pump and gently pump out the contents.

2 Put 2 tablespoons of logwood dye in a pan three-quarters full of water and boil for ten minutes to release the colour. Add the egg to the pan and ensure it is fully covered.

3 Remove the egg from the pan with a slotted spoon and rinse it under cold running water. Leave it to dry.

4 Using a white pencil, draw the design on the egg. You don't have to add all the details at this point.

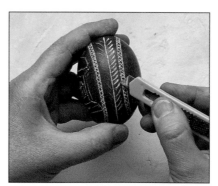

5 Using a craft knife, scratch away the border design – two sets of parallel lines with cross-hatching between each and a branch with leaves running down the centre of the border.

6 Scratch the outline of the house, embellishing the design as you go along. Add the stars above the door and over the roof. Repeat the design on the other side of the egg.

BRIGHT BUTTERFLIES

A combination of painting and scratching is used to decorate these eggs with their pretty, brightly coloured butterflies. It is important to use good acrylic paints with enough pigment so that only one coat is necessary. The final detailing is done by scratching, so the initial painting need not be perfect.

EQUIPMENT AND MATERIALS
- WHITE DUCK EGGS, BLOWN
- SHARP PENCIL
- ACRYLIC PAINT: YELLOW, RED, ORANGE, PURPLE AND BLUE
- FINE PAINTBRUSH
- CRAFT KNIFE

1 Draw the outline of the butterfly on the egg in pencil.

2 Paint the top wings and the tips of the lower wings yellow.

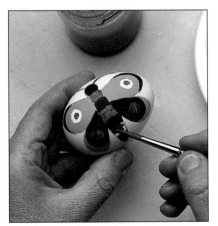

3 Paint the lower wings and the tips of the upper wings red. Paint orange dots in the centre of each wing. Paint purple and orange stripes on the body and orange antennae.

4 Paint the background and the circle outlines on the top wings blue. ▶

5 Use a craft knife, with the blade only slightly extended, to scratch away at the outline between the colours.

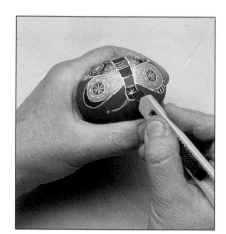

6 Scratch on the pattern of cross-hatching, dots, dashes and star as shown in the photograph. Scratch a thin line over the antennae ending with a dot.

QUAILS' EGGS WREATH

This charming little wreath is something to treasure for ever. It is a subtle combination of speckled quails' eggs threaded alongside similar eggs which have been masked with dots and dyed in a deep purple logwood dye. The tiny purple feathers stuck in place between the eggs beautifully complement the natural colours. Quails' eggs are very fragile so take great care when blowing them. Don't use an egg blowing kit, but just make a hole in both ends and blow the contents out gently into a bowl. The holes only need to be wide enough to thread on to a fairly fine wire.

EQUIPMENT AND MATERIALS

- 16 QUAILS' EGGS, BLOWN
- MASKING FLUID
- FINE PAINTBRUSH
- 1 TABLESPOON LOGWOOD DYE
- STAINLESS STEEL SAUCEPAN
- SLOTTED SPOON
- KITCHEN PAPER
- COPPER WIRE, ABOUT 70 CM (27½ IN)
- 16 PURPLE FEATHERS
- PVA (WHITE) GLUE

1 Paint dots on to eight of the eggs with the masking fluid. Leave to dry thoroughly.

2 Mix the logwood dye in a pan half-full of water. Boil for five to ten minutes, then remove from the heat. Place the masked eggs in the pan for a few minutes only (they take up the colour very quickly). Remove from the pan and pull the masking fluid from each egg. Leave to dry on kitchen paper.

3 Thread the masked eggs on to the copper wire alternating with the plain eggs. Twist the ends of the wire together to make a circle.

4 Dip the end of each feather into PVA glue and push into the hole at the top of each egg.

GLITTERY DECOUPAGE

These richly decorated eggs are really made of wood and the glittery papers have been saved from chocolate Easter egg wrappers! Sweet wrappers are also ideal, so keep your eyes open for anything interesting or suitable. You may need to adjust the template to fit your size of egg, or you may like to experiment with different papers and patterns.

EQUIPMENT AND MATERIALS

- GLITTERY PAPER, IN CONTRASTING COLOURS
- SCISSORS
- SELECTION OF WOODEN EGGS
- PVA (WHITE) GLUE
- PAINTBRUSH

1 Trace the template from the back of the book, enlarging or reducing it to fit your egg. Place the template over the glittery paper and cut around it. Cut out some contrasting colours to give a striped effect.

2 Paint a thin layer of glue on to the egg, slightly larger than the piece of paper to be stuck.

3 Lay the paper in place, matching the ends with the ends of the egg. Smooth it down to stick in place.

4 Carry on sticking down the paper shapes in this way using alternate contrasting colours.

GOOSE JUGS

These wonderful little jugs made from blown goose eggs have been directly inspired by rare examples found in Polish folk art. The eggs are rather cleverly disguised and it takes people some time to discover what the jugs are really made of. The brightly coloured paper-cut designs are very typical of Polish folk art and work particularly well as decorations on the surface of an egg. They look best when a number of them are displayed together in a row, perhaps on a kitchen dresser.

EQUIPMENT AND MATERIALS
- SHARP PENCIL
- GOOSE EGGS, BLOWN
- ORIGAMI PAPER: DARK AND LIGHT BLUE, BROWN AND ORANGE
- SCISSORS
- READY-MIXED WALLPAPER PASTE (FUNGICIDE-FREE)
- PINKING SHEARS
- THIN CARD (STOCK)
- PVA (WHITE) GLUE

▶

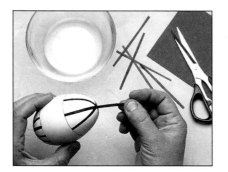

1 Draw pencil lines widthways around the egg to make a band of about 3.5 cm (1½ in) in the centre. Cut 16 strips of dark blue paper 3 mm (⅛ in) wide and long enough to reach from the pencil line, over the ends of the egg and down to the pencil line again. Stick in place with wallpaper paste.

2 Cut along one edge of a piece of brown paper with pinking shears. Using plain scissors, cut two strips 5 mm (³⁄₁₆ in) wide and long enough to fit around the egg widthways. Cut two strips of orange paper with straight edges 3 mm (⅛ in) wide and long enough to fit around the egg widthways.

3 Paste these strips on the egg to cover the blue strips, with the orange strip over the brown strip. Paste a light blue strip around the centre of the egg and stick four equidistant orange flowers around this strip. Add yellow and brown centres to the flowers and two-tone blue leaves.

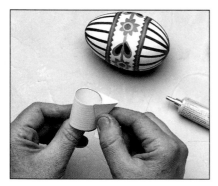

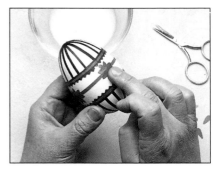

4 Trace the templates from the back of the book and cut them out of thin card. Using PVA glue, stick the spout section to the cylindrical neck. Leave to dry thoroughly before cutting away the card between the neck and spout.

5 Cover the base and spout with brown paper and decorate with orange strips cut with pinking shears. Put the base over the larger end of the egg and secure it by pasting strips of orange paper inside the base and over the bottom of the egg. Repeat with the spout.

6 Cut a 10 cm (4 in) strip of card for the handle and paste on a winding strip of dark blue paper. Stick the handle on to the neck and cover the join with matching paper. Bring the handle round and secure it to the brown-orange border in the same way.

BEADED EGGS

This project produces a stunning effect which is more commonly found in embroidery, but which is superbly adapted to adorn the perfect form of an egg. A polystyrene egg is used to great effect as part of the technique involves fixing the beads in place with pins. The eggs will last for ever, and they look quite beautiful displayed together in a glass or lustre bowl to show off their glittering iridescence.

EQUIPMENT AND MATERIALS
- FINE BLACK MARKER PEN
- POLYSTYRENE (STYROFOAM) EGGS
- DRESSMAKER'S PINS
- BEADS: BRIGHT BLUE, GOLD AND PURPLE
- PVA (WHITE) GLUE
- PAINTBRUSH
- SILVER JEWELLERY WIRE
- SCISSORS

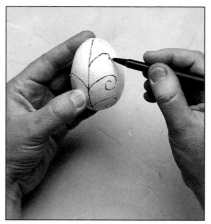

1 Using the marker pen, divide the egg into four sections lengthways, then draw three scrolls either side of one central line.

2 Using pins, fix two rows of blue beads along the vertical line.

3 Stick one row of blue beads along the scrolls.

4 Paint the area between the blue beads with PVA glue. Pick up the gold beads one by one with a pin and stick them into the glued area. Repeat this process with the back of the egg. ▶

5 To make the leaves, take two 25 cm (10 in) lengths of wire and thread a purple bead in the middle. Bend the ends forward and thread a bright blue bead on one side and a blue and a purple bead on the other side. Thread back the wire and pull tightly so these three beads appear on a double wire.

6 Continue thus, keeping a purple bead in the centre, but increasing and decreasing the number of blue beads to make the leaf shape. Twist the stems of the two leaves together and cut them off, leaving 1 cm (½ in). Make a hole in the top of the egg, dip the stem in PVA glue and push it into the hole. Leave to dry.

PAPER-CUTTING

*P*aper-cutting – or the art of Scherenschnitte – is a particularly well-known folk craft from Switzerland. Very intricate symmetrical designs are cut from a folded piece of black paper. They usually depict the natural world and village life. This beautiful craft can be easily adapted and applied to the curved surface of an egg as the intricate cutting means that the paper-cut is very flexible.

EQUIPMENT AND MATERIALS
- SCISSORS
- BLACK CRAFT PAPER
- PINKING SHEARS
- WHITE HENS' EGGS, BLOWN
- READY-MIXED WALLPAPER PASTE (FUNGICIDE-FREE)
- PAINTBRUSH
- PAPER CLIP
- ACRYLIC VARNISH

1 With normal scissors cut one strip of paper 2 mm (⅛ in) wide. Using the pinking shears, cut two strips 2 mm (⅛ in) wide and long enough to fit around the egg lengthways.

2 Smear wallpaper paste round the long side of the egg and on the paper strips. Stick the strips to the egg as shown above. Trace the template from the back of the book.

3 Cut a piece of paper 10 cm x 10 cm (4 in x 4 in) and fold it in half. Place the straight side of the template against the fold and secure it with a paperclip. Cut around the template and remove it.

4 Smear wallpaper paste on the side of the egg and the back of the paper cutout. Place it centrally on the egg and smooth it out carefully. Repeat with the other side. Leave to dry before coating the egg with acrylic varnish.

EMBROIDERY THREAD EGGS

Inspired by the traditional peasant method of decorating eggs in beautiful patterns made from the pith of reeds and rushes, these blown eggs are wound around in stripes and spirals using cotton embroidery threads. Once you become adept at this satisfying technique, invent some more intricate designs. Because the eggs are blown, they are light and they make an unusual hanging decoration for a branch of blossom in springtime.

EQUIPMENT AND MATERIALS
- PVA (WHITE) GLUE
- PAINTBRUSH
- HENS' EGGS, BLOWN
- EMBROIDERY THREADS: LIGHT BLUE, YELLOW, ORANGES, GREY AND PURPLE
- SCISSORS
- NEEDLE

1 Paint a small circle of glue on to the middle of the side of the egg. Press the end of the blue thread on to the middle of the glue and begin to wind it round in a tight spiral.

2 Continue the spiral with yellow thread and shades of orange to make a "target". Add more glue as needed.

3 Make another "target" on the other side with a yellow centre, then add grey and blue rings.

4 Apply glue to the surface between the two "targets" and wind the purple thread into this area. As the area is uneven, you will have to use a needle to double the thread back on itself.

GEOMETRIC GILDING

These rich metallic-effect eggs are decorated with gold and silver gilt cream. This is basically a soft wax which has been pigmented with metal powders. It can be polished with a soft cloth to produce a lovely subdued shine. The eggs look quite stunning when suspended from the branches of freshly gathered pussy willow in early spring.

EQUIPMENT AND MATERIALS
- HENS' EGGS, BLOWN
- LIGHT BLUE ACRYLIC PAINT
- FLAT PAINTBRUSH
- WHITE PENCIL
- GILT CREAM: GOLD AND SILVER
- SOFT CLOTH
- WIRE EGG HOLDERS

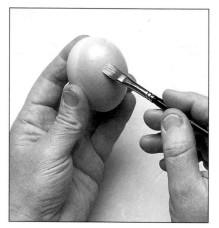

1 Paint the egg blue. This will have to be done in two stages, allowing one half of the egg to dry before painting the other half.

2 Draw white horizontal and vertical lines over the egg to make a large checked pattern.

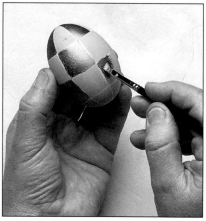

3 Paint the gold gilt cream in alternate squares, taking care to keep the edges neat. Leave to dry for about ten minutes.

4 Paint the silver squares in the same way, making sure that the joint between the two colours is very neat. Leave to dry for about ten minutes.

5 Polish the egg lightly with a soft cloth; the shine will deepen the longer you polish. Don't worry if some of the blue is revealed as this adds to the effect.

6 Hold the two prongs of the wire holder firmly together and push them into the hole at the top of the egg.

GILDED OSTRICH EGG

With a bit of searching it is quite possible to find a blown ostrich egg. Antique markets or junk shops are good places to look and this example was found in a decorative house-style shop. They are extraordinary objects with their finely textured ivory-coloured surface. They are immensely strong and it is said they can take the weight of a person if stood upon. The gilding on this egg has been done over a relief design first modelled in an all-purpose resin substance.

EQUIPMENT AND MATERIALS
- OSTRICH EGG, BLOWN
- DOUBLE-SIDED TAPE
- SOFT PENCIL
- ALL-PURPOSE RESIN
- KITCHEN KNIFE
- RED BOLE OR RED-OXIDE GESSO
- FINE PAINTBRUSH
- JAPAN GOLD SIZE
- GOLD LEAF, CUT INTO SQUARES
- SOFT PAINTBRUSH

1 Trace the template from the back of the book and place it centrally on the egg. Tape it in place and draw around it with a soft pencil to transfer the design.

2 Mix the all-purpose resin according to the manufacturer's instructions and press small amounts into the pencil outline. To make the stems, roll short lengths and press them in place. Use a knife to remove any excess.

3 Smooth the motif out with wet fingertips and wipe the egg clean. Make the leaf veins by pressing with a knife. Leave to dry thoroughly.

4 Paint the motif with red bole, taking care not to get any paint on the egg itself. Leave to dry for about 30 minutes. ▶

5 Paint on a layer of gold size. When it is almost dry, but still tacky, stick the small squares of gold leaf all over the motif, metal-side down. Leave to dry overnight.

6 Brush off any excess gold using a soft dry brush.

TEMPLATES

If you need to make these templates larger or smaller, to fit your eggs, you can use a photocopier to adjust them to the size you need or you can scale them up or down using a grid: draw a rectangle or square to the nearest 2.5 cm (1 in) round the template. Divide it into 2.5 cm (1 in) squares. On another piece of paper, draw another box as large as you want, but in proportion to the first box. Divide it into even squares. Copy the template into the large box, using the squares to guide you.

GILDED
OSTRICH EGG

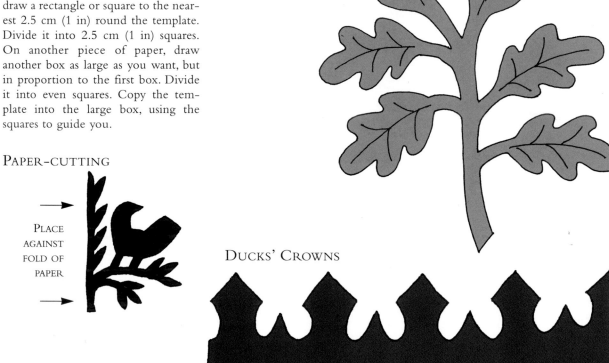

PAPER-CUTTING

PLACE
AGAINST
FOLD OF
PAPER

DUCKS' CROWNS

GLITTERY
DECOUPAGE

DIP-DYED TARTAN

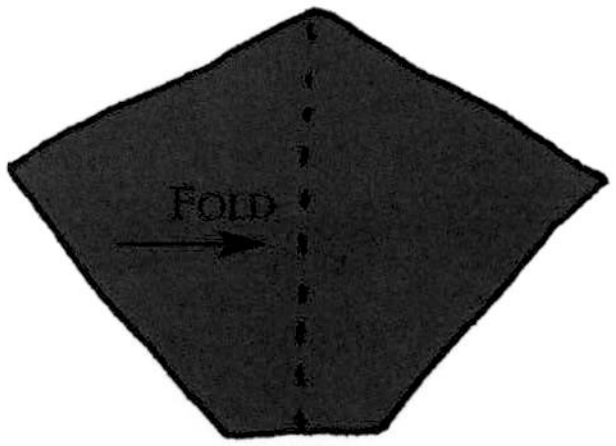

GOOSE JUGS

FOLD

SUPPLIERS

UK
Alec Tiranti, 27 Warren Street, London W1P 5DG
Tel. 020 7636 7887
For gold leaf, gold size, red bole, gilt cream and copper
wire and foil. Mail order available.

Panduro Hobby, FREEPOST, Transport House
Brentford, Middlesex TW8 8BR, Tel. 020 8847 6161
Mail order for egg dyes, eggs and all things to do with
egg decorating.

CANADA
Abby Arts & Crafts, 4118 Hastings Street, Burnaby, B C
Tel. 604 299 5201

Lewis Craft
2300 Younge Street, Toronto, Ont., Tel. 483 2783
Gold leaf, beads, copper wire, natural dyes, acrylic paints.

AUSTRALIA
Eggshell Artistry Supplies
198 Ramsay Street, Toowoomba
Queensland 4350
Tel. 076 36 2426
Mail order eggshells, paints, glues.

Norma Young
P O Box 233, Gympie, Queensland 4570
Tel. 074 829 667
Mail order findings, stands, beads.

USA
Pearl Paint Co.
308 Canal Street, New York, NY 10013
(212) 431-7932, (800) 221-6845
Paint and gilding supplies

Createx Colors
14 Airport Park Road
East Granby, CT 06026
(203) 653-5505; (800) 243-2712
Dyes

INDEX

ACKNOWLEDGEMENTS

With special thanks to Regula Ernst-Schneebeli for her invaluable research help in Switzerland; Heini Schneebeli for his care and attention in producing the lovely photographs, and to Olive Markham for sharing her long experience and knowledge of egg and hen varieties. Many thanks to George at Continental Stores for allowing me to pick out the best eggs in the shop, and to my children, Hannah and Rafi, who have consumed countless eggs without complaint over the last months.